DHEERAJ KAPOOR

THE TRAGEDY OF
JULIUS CAESAR

A GUIDE TO SHAKESPEARE'S PLAY

CHARACTERS

Flavius and Marullus — Flavius and Marullus are tribunes who wish to protect the common people from Caesar's tyranny. They break up a crowd of commoners waiting to welcome Caesar as he returns to Rome after a war. Flavius and Marullus are punished during the feast of Lupercal for removing ornaments from Caesar's statues.

Julius Caesar — Julius Caesar is a successful military leader who wants to become ruler of Rome. Julius Caesar is easily flattered, and overly ambitious. He is assassinated in the middle of the play. Later, Caesar's spirit appears to Brutus at Sardis and at Philippi.

Julius Caesar is an ambitious man who wishes to soar above the view of men. He commands loyalty and respect through fear. Caesar thinks of himself as a god. He does not fear men like Cassius because he believes that he is untouchable and higher in status than regular men. Although he portrays an image of immortality and strength, Julius Caesar has his weaknesses. As he leaves the stage after the Lupercal celebrations, he asks Antony to speak on his right side because he is deaf in his left ear.

When we realize that he is partially deaf, we see a contrast between the people's idea of Caesar as a vain, god-like character and a frail, aging man who is in danger of being assassinated.

Julius Caesar is also an arrogant man. Although he shows himself to be superstitious, he ignores the omens that foretell his death. He believes death cannot be avoided. However, he does not think that his own death is even possible.

Caesar sees himself as infallible and says that any threats to his life vanish when they look upon his face. He even considers himself more dangerous than Danger.

Julius Caesar thinks of himself as superior to regular mortals. He does not believe that he, like all humans is also vulnerable. Caesar ignores Calpurnia and the soothsayer's warnings and does not read Artemidorus' letter because he thinks he is undefeatable.

Casca — Casca watches Caesar as he tries to convince the people of Rome to offer him the crown. He reports Caesar's failure to Brutus and Cassius. Casca joins the conspiracy the night before the assassination and is the first conspirator to stab Caesar.

Calpurnia — Calpurnia is a noble Roman woman. She is the wife of Julius Caesar. She has an affectionate relationship with her husband and is concerned for his safety. She urges Caesar to stay at home on the ides of March. She believes the unnatural events of the previous night are an omen of danger. Calpurnia also has a prophetic dream in which she sees Caesar's body spouting blood.

Marcus Antonius (Mark Antony) — Mark Antony is a confidant and a devoted follower of Caesar. He offers Caesar a crown during the feast of Lupercal. Antony enjoys a life of splendor and comfort, but he is also an accomplished military general. Antony is an experienced politician and is skilled at public speaking. He is able to convince Brutus to allow him to speak at Caesar's funeral. With his passionate funeral speech, Antony succeeds in persuading the common people to rebel against the conspirators. He is one of the triumvirs, and he and Octavius defeat Brutus and Cassius at Philippi. We also see Mark Antony as cold-hearted and selfish. This is evident in the way Antony thinks of Lepidus. He is willing to use Lepidus to accomplish his goals, before casting him aside. Antony also does not hesitate to murder anyone who may prove dangerous to him.

Soothsayer — The soothsayer is a character who tries to warn Caesar of his impending death. He calls to Caesar during the celebration of the feast of Lupercal and warns him to "beware the ides of March." He again warns Caesar as he enters the Capitol.

Marcus Brutus — Brutus is a *praetor* or judicial magistrate of Rome. He is admired for his noble nature. He joins the conspiracy because he fears that Caesar will become a tyrant. While his intentions are noble, Brutus makes various bad decisions. Brutus defeats Octavius' army in the first battle at Philippi. However, he loses the second battle and commits suicide rather than be captured.

Brutus comes across as the most complex character in the play. He is proud of being considered as honorable and noble. However, Brutus is also naïve in his behavior and thinking.

Brutus holds such a good reputation in Roman society that Cassius and the other conspirators believe that Brutus' reputation and involvement will make the conspiracy seem honorable.

Brutus is also unable to fully understand the true motives of Cassius and Antony. He seems gullible when he agrees to join the conspiracy. He believes that all the conspirators are acting out of honor and have noble intentions.

Brutus does not see Antony's true intentions when he asks permission to speak at Caesar's funeral. He underestimates Antony's power and influence over the people. He is mistaken when he thinks Antony is only a limb of Caesar and will not have much influence after Caesar's death.

Brutus does not make important decisions after careful thought and consideration. He takes control of the conspiracy and makes hasty decisions about the fate of Antony. He does not really form a plan to take control of the government after the assassination. He makes a fatal mistake when he allows Antony to speak at the funeral. By doing this, he allows Antony to completely turn the people of Rome against the conspirators.

Throughout the play, Brutus finds it difficult to justify the assassination of Caesar.

The appearance of Caesar's ghost to Brutus in Sardis and at Philippi signifies that Brutus has not been able to come to terms with his participation in the conspiracy.

His final words can be understood almost as a plea. Brutus seems to be pleading for an end to his inner conflict about whether the conspiracy was justified.

Cassius — Cassius is Brutus' brother-in-law. He is able to accurately judge human character. Cassius plans the conspiracy against Caesar and cunningly convinces Brutus to join his cause. He convinces Brutus by flattering him and taking advantage of his weaknesses. Cassius does not agree that Antony should be allowed to live once Caesar is dead. He also correctly assumes that Antony will encourage the people to rebel if he is allowed to speak at Caesar's funeral. Cassius is defeated by Antony in the first battle of Philippi. He commits suicide when he mistakenly believes that Brutus has been defeated.

Cicero — Cicero is a senator and a famous orator of Rome. He is calm and philosophical when he meets Casca on the night before the day of Caesar's assassination. The triumvirs have him killed.

Cinna — Cinna is the conspirator who encourages Cassius to make noble Brutus join the conspiracy. Cinna helps convince Brutus by placing some of Cassius' forged letters in places where Brutus will find them.

Lucius — Lucius is Brutus' young servant. Brutus treats him well with kindness and tolerance.

Decius Brutus — Decius Brutus is the conspirator who convinces Caesar to attend the Senate on the day of the ides of March when he realizes that Caesar is not willing to leave his house. Decius flatters Caesar by interpreting Calpurnia's nightmare. Decius knows exactly how to persuade Caesar and does this by telling Caesar that the Senate plans to crown him king.

Metellus Cimber — Metellus Cimber is the conspirator who attracts Caesar's attention when he enters the Capitol. Cimber distracts Caesar by requesting him to reverse his brother's banishment. This allows the assassins to surround Caesar, giving Casca a chance to stab him from behind.

Trebonius — Trebonius is one of the conspirators who agree with Brutus that Antony should not be killed alongside Caesar. Trebonius takes Antony out of the Capitol so that he does not interfere with assassination of Caesar. Therefore, Trebonius is the only conspirator who does not actually stab Caesar.

Portia — Portia is the strong and devoted wife of Brutus. She is the daughter of Marcus Cato. Her act of self-injury during the play shows her as a brave woman. By this act, she proves to Brutus that she is worthy of hearing his secrets. Although she shows that she has a strong mind, Portia admits on the morning of the assassination, that she has a woman's strength. After hearing Brutus' plans, she finds it difficult to conceal his secrets because she is extremely concerned for his safety. She commits suicide when she finds out that Brutus' army is no match for Octavius and Antony's.

Caius Ligarius — Caius Ligarius does not support Caesar. Although he has been unwell, Ligarius is inspired by Brutus' noble character to forget his illness and participate in the conspiracy. He sees Brutus as a leader and is willing to follow him. Ligarius joins the conspirators in the early morning of the ides of March.

Publius — Publius is an elderly senator. He arrives with the conspirators to lead Caesar to the Capitol. He is stunned as he witnesses Caesar's assassination. Brutus sends Publius out into the streets to tell the people of Rome that no one else will be harmed.

Artemidorus — Artemidorus is a teacher of rhetoric. He was friends with many of the conspirators and therefore knows about the conspiracy. Artemidorus is one of Caesar's well-wishers. He gives Caesar a letter just before he enters the Capitol. In the letter, Artemidorus names the conspirators and writes that they intend to kill Caesar. However, Caesar does not read Artemidorus' letter.

Popilius Lena — Popilius Lena is a senator who wishes Cassius well in his "enterprise" as Caesar enters the Capitol. This comment increases the dramatic tension in the moments before the assassination. Popilius' words make Cassius and Brutus doubt whether the conspiracy has been discovered.

Cinna the Poet — Cinna the poet is caught in the riot after Antony's funeral speech. He is going to attend Caesar's funeral, when he is attacked by the angry mob. Cinna's attackers confuse him with Cinna the conspirator. However, even after they discover that he is not a conspirator, but a poet, they kill him anyway "for his bad verses".

Octavius Caesar — Octavius Caesar is the adopted son and heir of Julius Caesar. He is one of the triumvirs who rule Rome after the death of Julius Caesar. He and Antony lead the army to victory against Cassius and Brutus at Philippi.

Octavius is able to understand that not all who act friendly are actually friends. He is wary of Antony because he realizes that Antony will seize power if given the chance. Octavius does not allow Antony to control him.

However, Octavius recognizes that Antony has considerable political and military experience. Therefore, he agrees when Antony makes Lepidus a junior partner in the triumvirate.

He also understands that Antony is right when he advises that the most important matter after Caesar's assassination is to confront the armies of Brutus and Cassius, and allow the enemy to start the battle.

Lepidus — Lepidus joins Antony and Octavius to form the Second Triumvirate to rule the Roman Empire after the assassination of Julius Caesar. As a man, Lepidus is weak, and Antony uses him to run errands.

Lucilius — Lucilius is the soldier who is mistaken for Brutus when he is captured by Antony's soldiers at the second battle of Philippi. Antony admires Lucilius' bravery and loyalty to Brutus and promises to protect him and treat him kindly. Antony hopes that Lucilius will serve him as loyally as he did Brutus, once the battle is over.

Pindarus — At Philippi, Pindarus makes a grave error that has a sad outcome. He wrongly tells his master, Cassius, that his soldier Titinius has been captured by the enemy. Titinius had actually been greeted by Brutus' victorious soldiers. Thinking that the entire battle is lost, Cassius decides to commit suicide. He commands Pindarus to kill him with the same sword that he used to help assassinate Caesar.

Titinius — Titinius is a soldier in Cassius and Brutus' army. He guards the tent at Sardis during the argument between Cassius and Brutus. Titinius is sent by Cassius at the end of the first battle to find out if the enemy was approaching. When he finds out that Cassius had committed suicide thinking that Titinius had been captured by the enemy, Titinius kills himself in despair over the loss of his friend.

Messala — Messala is a soldier in Brutus and Cassius' army. Messala gives reports on the armies of Antony and Octavius. He informs Brutus about Portia's death. At Philippi, Cassius confess to Messala that he does not think the battle will be successful for them. Messala later discovers Cassius' lifeless body.

Varro and Claudius — Varro and Cladius are Brutus' servants. They spend the night in Brutus' tent at Sardis. Neither of them sees the ghost of Caesar that appears to Brutus.

Young Cato — Young Cato is the son of Marcus Cato and Portia's brother. He is also Brutus' brother-in-law, and a soldier in Brutus and Cassius' army. Young Cato dies during the second battle at Philippi, trying to inspire the army.

Clitus and Dardanius — Clitus and Dardanius are Brutus' servants. They refuse their master's request, when he asks them to kill him at Philippi.

Volumnius — Volumnius is Brutus' friend and a soldier in his army at Philippi. He refuses to hold a sword for Brutus to impale himself on.

Strato — Strato is a loyal servant who holds Brutus' sword so that he can commit suicide. Later, Strato becomes a servant to Octavius.

ACT ONE

SCENE 1

On a street in ancient Rome, Flavius and Marullus, two Roman tribunes come across a group of workmen and ask them what they do for a living. They ask them to explain why they are not working. The first workman, a carpenter, answers straight forwardly, but the second workman answers with a pun, saying that he is a cobbler.

COBBLER A trade, sir, that I hope I may use with a safe conscience, which is, indeed, sir, a mender of bad soles.

When the cobbler tells Marullus that he is a cobbler, Marullus and Flavius misunderstand him and think he is a bungler, or an incompetent person. Flavius only understands later in this scene that the cobbler is actually a shoemaker.

There is a pun on the word 'soles' here which could also refer to people's 'souls'.

When the cobbler says he is a mender of bad soles, Marullus and Flavius again misunderstand him. This is because 'soles' sounds similar to 'souls'.

The cobbler says he and his fellow workmen have gathered to welcome Caesar and to rejoice in his triumph over Pompey.

MARULLUS	O you hard hearts, you cruel men of Rome,
	Knew you not Pompey? Many a time and oft
	Have you climb'd up to walls and battlements,
	To towers and windows, yea, to chimney-tops,
	Your infants in your arms, and there have sat
	The livelong day, with patient expectation,
	To see great Pompey pass the streets of Rome:
	And when you saw his chariot but appear,
	Have you not made an universal shout,
	That Tiber trembled underneath her banks,
	To hear the replication of your sounds
	Made in her concave shores?

Marullus calls the workmen "stones" and says they are "worse than senseless things". He says they are unfeeling, and accuses them of forgetting that they were disrespecting the great Pompey, whose triumphs they once cheered so enthusiastically. He reminds the workmen that when they caught sight of Pompey's chariot, they would shout so loud that the river Tiber shook as it echoed.

MARULLUS   And do you now put on your best
             attire?
             And do you now cull out a holiday?"
             And do you now strew flowers in his
             way
             That comes in triumph over Pompey's
             blood?
             Be gone!
             Run to your houses, fall upon your
             knees,
             Pray to the goods to Intermit the
             plague
             That needs must light on this
             ingratitude.

Marullus scolds the workmen for wanting to honor the man who is celebrating a victory in battle over Pompey's sons. He commands them to return to their homes to ask forgiveness of the gods for their ingratitude.

FLAVIUS   Go, Go, good countrymen, and for this
             fault,
             Assemble all the poor men of your sort,
             Draw them to Tiber banks, and weep
             your tears
             Into the channel till the lowest stream
             Do kiss the most exalted shores of all.

Flavius orders the workmen to assemble all the commoners they can and take them to the banks of the Tiber and fill the river with their tears of remorse for the dishonor they have shown Pompey.

FLAVIUS   Go you down that way towards the
Capitol.
This way will I. Disrobe the images
If you do find them decked with
ceremonies.

Flavius then tells Marullus to assist him in removing the ceremonial decorations that have been placed on public statues in honor of Caesar's triumph. Marullus wonders whether it is right to deface the statues on the day when the feast of Lupercal is being celebrated.

FLAVIUS   It is no matter. Let no images
Be hung with Caesar's trophies. I'll
about
And drive away the vulgar from the
streets.
So do you too, where you perceive
them thick.

Flavius tells Marullus that it doesn't matter if it is the feast of Lupercal. He tells Marullus to make sure that none of the statues are decorated to honor Caesar. He says he will walk around and make sure the commoners are not wandering in the street, while Marullus does the same.

FLAVIUS	These growing feathers plucked from Caesar's wing
	Will make him fly an ordinary pitch,
	Who else would soar above the view of men
	And keep us all in servile fearfulness.

Flavius says that they must remove the decorations to prevent Caesar from becoming a godlike tyrant. He says if they remove Caesar's support, he will come down to earth. Otherwise, he will think he is too important and he will keep the rest of the people in a state of fear and obedience.

As the play opens, the mood seems extremely repressive. Flavius and Marullus, tribunes of Rome, are attempting to reestablish civil order. There is disorder in the streets. The tribunes call upon the commoners to identify themselves in terms of their occupations. In the past, Flavius could recognize a man's status by his dress, but now all the signs of stability are gone and the world is out of control and dangerous. At first glance, this disorder is attributed to the lower classes who won't wear the signs of their trade and who taunt the tribunes with saucy language full of puns.

When Flavius demands, "Is this a holiday?" he questions whether Caesar's triumph ought to be celebrated. This a rhetorical question. Flavius thinks poor Romans ought not to celebrate but should weep tears into the river. Caesar, a member of the ruling class, has violently overthrown the government and brought civil strife with him. These issues would have resonated with an audience of Shakespeare's time as England was ruled by a Queen, who, by virtue of being a woman, was perceived as less able to rule than a man. (Ironically, Elizabeth I brought a great deal of peace and stability to England.) Statues of Caesar wearing a crown have been set up before he has been offered the position of ruler, and Flavius and Marullus plan to deface them. Flavius, by calling for Caesar's statues to be disrobed, seems to imply that Caesar has overstepped his bounds. Just as Caesar has brought disorder with him, the tribunes contribute to the upheaval by becoming part of the unruly mob themselves.

Pay close attention to the interactions between the nobles and the common people. While speaking to a cobbler, the way Marullus treats the commoner shows the unfair structure of society during that time. Another example of this is shown frequently throughout the scene where the cobbler must show respect by calling Marullus and Flavius "sir" and then is referred to as a man with no name.

When he admonishes the cobbler and the common people, Marullus shows his discriminatory attitude when he calls them "You blocks, you stones, you worse than senseless things!"

The statues of Caesar are significant because they are meant to establish a positive image of Caesar in the popular imagination. Romans generally associate statues with gods and important political figures. Thus, Caesar would take on the same associations. The act of erecting these statues is part of the process of persuasion and persuasion is a central theme of this play.

The splintering of the ruling class means that there is no longer one common vision of what Rome is and what it is to be a Roman. Marullus draws attention to this problem when he returns to Flavius' original question, "Is this a holiday?" As Marullus points out, it is indeed a holiday—the festival of Lupercal. He is concerned that, by disrobing the images of Caesar, he will destroy ceremonies meant not only to celebrate Caesar but also a festival that is part of Rome's history, tradition, and religion.

Ceremonies and rituals, in both Roman and Elizabethan terms, were a means of maintaining social order, of celebrating one's identity. By destroying that identity, Marullus seems to sense that he will contribute to the destruction of the state. His intuition is correct and foreshadows the battles to come.

SCENE 2

Caesar has entered Rome in triumph.

CAESAR   **Stand you directly in Antonius' way**
When he doth run his course. — Antonius!

Caesar calls to his wife, Calpurnia, and tells her to stand where
Mark Antony, who is going to run in the traditional footrace of
the Lupercal, can touch her as he passes.

CAESAR   **Forget not in your speed, Antonius,**
To touch Calpurnia, for our elders say
The barren, touchèd in this holy chase,
Shake off their sterile curse.

Caesar asks Antony to touch Calpurnia when he is running the
race because he believes that if a childless woman is touched by
one of the holy runners, she will lose her sterility.

Calpurnia, Caesar's wife, has not borne him any children, and
while in the Elizabethan mind the problem would have resided
with the woman, here, Caesar's virility is also being questioned.
By calling upon Antony, a man known for being athletic and a
womanizer, Caesar seems to imply that he is impotent.

SOOTHSAYER   Beware the ides of March.

A soothsayer calls from the crowd warning Caesar to "beware the ides of March". Caesar doesn't hear the man clearly, but others do. It is ironic that Brutus, who will be Caesar's murderer, repeats the soothsayer's words to Caesar.

BRUTUS   A soothsayer bids you beware the ides of March.

When Caesar asks to see the soothsayer's face, he approaches and repeats his warning.

CAESAR   He is a dreamer. Let us leave him. Pass!

Caesar pays no attention to the soothsayer's words and departs with his attendants, leaving Brutus and Cassius behind.

Caesar is often considered a superstitious man and therefore weak, but this is not really true. All the characters in this play believe in the supernatural. It is one of the play's themes that they all misinterpret and attempt to turn signs and omens to their own advantage. What characterizes Caesar as weak, is his susceptibility to flattering interpretations of omens and his inability to distinguish between good advice and bad, good advisors and bad. He fails to appreciate that those who surround him are not all supporters.

Cassius asks Brutus if he intends to watch the race and Brutus says that he doesn't like sports. Just as Brutus is about to leave, Cassius tells Brutus that he seems less affectionate towards him than usual.

BRUTUS   Cassius,
Be not deceived. If I have veiled my look,
I turn the of my countenance
Merely upon myself. Vexèd I am
Of late with passions of some difference,
Conceptions only proper to myself,
Which give some soil perhaps to my
behaviors.

Brutus tells Cassius not to be offended by his indifferent behavior. Brutus explains that he is troubled by inner conflicts that have affected his behavior.

CASSIUS   Tell me, good Brutus, can you see your face?

Cassius, who wants to overthrow Caesar, then tries to win Brutus' support and make him join his cause. By asking Brutus if he can see his face, Cassius means to ask if Brutus realizes his true worth.

Brutus replies that the eye cannot see itself, except if it is reflected in other surfaces.

CASSIUS   And it is very much lamented, Brutus,
That you have no such mirrors as will turn
Your hidden worthiness into your eye
That you might see your shadow. I have
heard
Where many of the best respect in Rome,
Except immortal Caesar, speaking of Brutus
And groaning underneath this age's yoke,
Have wished that noble Brutus had his eyes.

In these lines, Cassius tries to flatter Brutus. He says it is unfortunate that Brutus cannot see his hidden worthiness. Trying to win Brutus' support for the conspiracy, Cassius tells Brutus that he has heard many respected Romans speaking in praise of him and complaining about the tyranny of the government. He says that the people wished that Brutus could see the dangers of tyranny more clearly.

Cassius tries to flatter Brutus because he wants to know what Brutus feels about the idea of Caesar becoming a dictator in Rome.

BRUTUS   Into what dangers would you lead me,
Cassius,
That you would have me seek into myself
For that which is not in me?

Brutus asks Cassius what dangers he is trying to lead him into. He asks what qualities Cassius wants him to see in himself, that may not actually be there.

CASSIUS   Therefore, good Brutus, be prepared to hear.
And since you know you cannot see yourself
So well as by reflection, I, your glass,
Will modestly discover to yourself
That of yourself which you yet know not of.

Cassius tells Brutus that he will be like a mirror for Brutus so that Brutus can understand his true worthiness. Cassius says he will, like a mirror, show Brutus his true noble qualities, which he cannot see.

BRUTUS   What means this shouting? I do fear, the people
Choose Caesar for their king.

Brutus and Cassius hear a shout and Brutus asks why the people are shouting. He says that he is afraid that the people have made Caesar their king.

When Brutus reveals his fear in these lines, Cassius realizes that Brutus also might not want Caesar to be king.

Brutus agrees that he would not like to see Caesar as king but says that he loves Caesar.

CASSIUS   I cannot tell what you and other men
Think of this life, but, for my single self,
I had as life not be as live to be
In awe of such a thing as I myself.
I was born free as Caesar. So were you.

Through these lines, Cassius reminds Brutus that Caesar is simply a regular mortal like them, with ordinary human weaknesses. Cassius says that he would rather die than see such a man, as Caesar, become his master.

CASSIUS   **I, as Aeneas, our great ancestor,**
                   Did from the flames of Troy upon his
                   shoulder
                   The old Anchises bear, so from the waves of
                   Tiber
                   Did I the tired Caesar.

Cassius recounts saving Caesar from drowning to show Brutus that Caesar, like any other man, also has weaknesses. Cassius says that like how Aeneas, their great ancestor carried his old father Anchises on his shoulders and saved him from the flames of Troy, he too carried Caesar from the river.

CASSIUS   **And this man**
                   Is now become a god, and Cassius is
                   A wretched creature and must bend his body
                   If Caesar carelessly but nod on him.

Cassius speaks of how Caesar is seen as a god. Cassius says he is like a wretched creature who must bow to Caesar if he simply looks in his direction.

CASSIUS   **He had a fever when he was in Spain,**
                   And when the fit was on him, I did mark
                   How he did shake. 'Tis true, this god did
                   shake!

Here, Cassius describes the fever that left Caesar groaning and trembling as he had an epileptic fit. He says that Caesar, the god, shook. The same eyes whose gaze frightens the world became dull. Cassius reveals Caesar's weaknesses by saying that he begged for water like a sick girl.

Several times during their conversation, Cassius and Brutus hear shouts and the sounds of trumpets. Brutus again thinks that these shouts are applause for some new honors given to Caesar.

CASSIUS   **Why, man, he doth bestride the narrow world**
               Like a Colossus, and we petty men
               Walk under his huge legs and peep about
               To find ourselves dishonorable graves.
               Men at some time are masters of their fates.
               The fault, dear Brutus, is not in our stars
               But in ourselves, that we are underlings.

Cassius complains that Caesar seems to walk on earth like a giant while they are small men who walk in his shadow and can only expect to die without honor, as slaves. Cassius reminds Brutus that men can decide their fates. He says it is not destiny's fault, but our own fault that we are slaves.

CASSIUS   **Brutus and Caesar—what should be in that "Caesar"?**
               Why should that name be sounded more than yours?
               Write them together, yours is as fair a name.

Cassius questions what is so special about "Caesar"? He asks why should Caesar's name be proclaimed more than the name of Brutus? Brutus is just as good a name as Caesar.

CASSIUS   Conjure with 'em,
                  "Brutus" will start a spirit as soon as
                  "Caesar."
                  Now in the names of all the gods at once,
                  Upon what meat doth Caesar feed
                  That he is grown so great?

Cassius tells Brutus that if you cast a spell with the name of Caesar and Brutus, "Brutus" is equally capable of commanding as much respect as Caesar. The name "Brutus" will also be able to call up a ghost like the name "Caesar" can. He asks Brutus, what different food does Caesar eat that has made him so great?

Cassius says that now, in Rome, there seems to be place only for one man. Nobody else except Caesar is of any importance.

CASSIUS   Oh, you and I have heard our fathers say,
                  There was a Brutus once that would have
                  brooked
                  Th' eternal devil to keep his state in Rome
                  As easily as a king.

In these lines, Cassius reminds Brutus of Brutus' noble ancestry. He wants to tell Brutus that the people, his fellow Romans, expect Brutus to serve his country like his ancestors did. He says that another Brutus — Brutus' ancestor — would have done everything he could to preserve democracy in Rome before he let a tyrant gain absolute power over the people.

When he sees how Brutus reacts to his words, Cassius thinks that Brutus might be convinced to join the conspiracy against Caesar.

Caesar returns from the games with his attendants.

CAESAR   Let me have men about me that are fat,
Sleek-headed men and such as sleep a-nights.
Yond Cassius has a lean and hungry look.
He thinks too much. Such men are
dangerous.

Caesar tells Mark Antony that he feels suspicious of Cassius. Caesar is unhappy when he sees Cassius lurking in the corner. Caesar is disturbed by Cassius because he cannot corrupt him with lavish comforts. He thinks Cassius is a dangerous man because he has a "lean and hungry look". Caesar prefers to have fat, lazy men around him, who are corrupt and who will not threaten his leadership. Caesar believes that men like Cassius are over ambitious.

CAESAR   Would he were fatter! But I fear him not.
Yet if my name were liable to fear,
I do not know the man I should avoid
So soon as that spare Cassius. He reads
much.
He is a great observer, and he looks
Quite through the deeds of men.

In these lines, Caesar makes an appropriate analysis of Cassius' character. He says he was not afraid of Cassius, although if he had to fear any man, he would be wary of Cassius. Caesar understands that Cassius is a keen observer who can see a person's hidden motives.

CAESAR   Such men as he be never at heart's ease
               Whiles they behold a greater than themselves,
               And therefore are they very dangerous.

Caesar tells Antony that men like Cassius will not be comfortable when they are ruled by someone who ranks higher than themselves. According to Caesar, men like Cassius like to be in positions of power and authority. This is why he finds Cassius to be dangerous.

As he leaves the stage, Caesar shows one of his weaknesses. He tells Antony to shift over to his right side because he is deaf in his left ear and cannot hear. Caesar and Antony leave while Antony tries to calm Caesar's fears about Cassius. Antony reassures Caesar by saying that Cassius is an honorable Roman and is not dangerous.

As Caesar exits, Brutus and Cassius stop Casca and speak with him. They ask him what happened at the games.

CASCA   Why, there was a crown offered him; and
               being offered him, he put it by with the back
               of his hand, thus; and then the people fell a-
               shouting.

Casca tells them that Mark Antony offered the crown to Caesar three times, but that Caesar rejected it each time.

Casca tells Cassius and Brutus that he thinks Caesar was pretending not to want the crown. The people were shouting and cheering at the drama that was unfolding in front of them.

However, Caesar believed the people were cheering for him, expecting him to accept the crown.

CASSIUS   But soft, I pray you. What, did Caesar swoon?

Casca then tells Brutus and Cassius that after he refused the crown for the third time, Caesar fainted, foamed at the mouth and fell to the ground in the marketplace. Brutus then says that Caesar has "the falling sickness", epilepsy.

Cassius invites Casca to have dinner with him because he wants to try and get Casca to join the conspiracy. Casca declines the invitation and leaves.

CASSIUS   Well, Brutus, thou art noble. Yet I see
Thy honorable mettle may be wrought
From that it is disposed.

When Casca and Brutus have gone, Cassius in a brief soliloquy indicates his plans to convince Brutus to join the conspiracy against Caesar. Cassius understands that Brutus has noble intentions that can be taken advantage of.

CASSIUS   I will this night,
In several hands, in at his windows throw,
As if they came from several citizens,
Writings all tending to the great opinion
That Rome holds of his name, wherein
obscurely
Caesar's ambition shall be glancèd at.

Cassius believes that he can trick Brutus into joining the conspiracy. He decides to throw into Brutus' window, a few letters, written in different handwriting. When Brutus sees these letters, he will believe that they came from different citizens, who write to praise him and complain about Caesar's growing ambition.

SCENE 3

Scene 3 opens with nature reflecting the unrest and troubles in Rome. That evening, Cicero and Casca meet on a street in Rome. There has been a terrible storm.

CASCA   Are not you moved when all the sway of earth
                   Shakes like a thing inform? O Cicero,
                   I have seen tempests when the scolding winds
                   Have rived the knotty oaks, and I have seen
                   Th' ambitious ocean swell and rage and foam
                   To be exalted with the threatening clouds,
                   But never till tonight, never till now,
                   Did I go through a tempest dropping fire.

Casca asks Cicero if he was disturbed by the storm that night. Casca says he has seen storms in which angry winds destroyed old oak trees. He has also seen the ocean rage as though it wanted to reach the storm clouds. But never before this night has he seen a storm that drops fire.

CASCA   Against the Capitol I met a lion,
Who glared upon me and went surly by,
Without annoying me. And there were drawn
Upon a heap a hundred ghastly women,
Transformèd with their fear, who swore they saw
Men all in fire walk up and down the streets.

Casca describes to Cicero the unnatural sights that he has seen. He has seen a lion in front of the Capitol, and he told Cicero that he had seen frightened women who said they had seen men on fire walk in the streets.

CASCA   And yesterday the bird of night did sit
Even at noon-day upon the marketplace,
Hooting and shrieking. When these prodigies
Do so conjointly meet, let no men say,
"These are their reasons. They are natural."
For I believe they are portentous things
Unto the climate that they point upon.

Casca also tells Cicero that he saw an owl hooting in the marketplace at noon. Casca feels that these unnatural sights cannot be explained. He thinks these strange sights are omens of trouble for Rome.

Cicero agrees that it is a strange time, but says men will interpret things however it suits them and may misunderstand the actual meaning of things. Before he leaves, he asks Casca if Caesar will visit the Capitol the next day.

CASSIUS   You are dull, Casca, and those sparks of life
           That should be in a Roman you do want,
           Or else you use not. You look pale, and gaze,
           And put on fear, and cast yourself in wonder
           To see the strange impatience of the heavens.

Cassius enters and interprets the strange sights and omens to suit his own purposes. He tells Casca that he has not understood the true meaning of these strange sights. Cassius says that Casca should think like a true Roman who has quick wit. He interprets the supernatural happenings as divine warnings that Caesar threatens to destroy the Republic.

CASSIUS   Now could I, Casca, name to thee a man
           Most like this dreadful night,
           That thunders, lightens, opens graves, and
           roars
           As doth the lion in the Capitol.

Cassius tells Casca that he could name a man who behaved like this dreadful night—a man who splits open graves and roars like the lion in the Capitol. He says this man, Caesar, has become too powerful, and almost larger than life.

CASSIUS   I know where I will wear this dagger then.
           Cassius from bondage will deliver Cassius.
           Therein, he gods, you make the weak most
           strong.

When Casca tells him that the senators plan to crown Caesar king the next day at the Capitol, Cassius says he would kill himself if

Caesar became king. Cassius says suicide would save him from slavery.

CASSIUS   **And why should Caesar be a tyrant then?**
Poor man! I know he would not be a wolf
But that he sees the Romans are but sheep.

Cassius says Caesar would not have become a tyrant. He says Caesar believed the Romans were like sheep. He says Caesar would not be a lion if the Roman people were not such helpless creatures. By saying this about Caesar, Cassius tries to convince Casca to work with him against Caesar.

Casca agrees to join the conspiracy against Caesar. He tells Cassius that if they were working together to free the people of Rome from a tyrant like Caesar, then he will willingly do what he can to help.

Cassius then tells Casca that he had convinced other noble Romans to join the conspiracy and they were all meeting outside Pompey's theatre on this frightening night, to discuss the work they have to do. Cassius tells Cassius their task was as fiery and terrible as the sky on that night.

CASSIUS   **Good Cinna, take this paper,**
And look you lay it in the praetor's chair
Where Brutus may but find it. And throw this
In at his window.

When Cinna, another conspirator, joins them, Cassius asks him to leave a paper in the judge's chair where Brutus may find it. Cassius also tells Cinna to throw a message through Brutus' window. Cassius hopes these messages will convince Brutus to join the conspiracy against Caesar. Cassius then tells Cinna to come to Pompey's theatre where the other conspirators — Decius Brutus, Trebonius, and Metellus Cimber — are meeting.

CASCA   **Oh, he sits high in all the people's hearts,**
And that which would appear offence in us,
His countenance, like richest alchemy,
Will change to virtue and to worthiness.

Casca correctly says that the Roman people love Brutus and have a lot of respect for him. He says if they acted against Caesar without Brutus' support, their actions would look bad. However, if Brutus joined the conspiracy, his actions even if they were bad, would look noble and honorable. Casca compares Brutus' character to an alchemist who turns tin to valuable gold.

Act I ends in gloom and darkness with the state beginning to splinter. The daylight that Cassius perceives on the horizon is, paradoxically, a light that will show the cracks all the more clearly.

ACT TWO

SCENE 1

Act Two opens in Brutus' orchard. It is night and Brutus is unable to sleep. He is walking in his orchard. He is thinking about his conversation with Cassius. Brutus is torn between his love for Caesar and his fear that Caesar's unlimited power will destroy the Republic.

He calls impatiently for his servant, Lucius, and sends him to light a candle in his study.

BRUTUS   It must be by his death, and for my part
I know no personal cause to spurn at him
But for the general. He would be crowned.
How that might change his nature, there's
the question.
It is the bright day that brings forth the adder
And that craves wary walking. Crown him
that,
And then I grant we put a sting in him
That at his will he may do danger with.

When he is alone, Brutus speaks one of the most important and controversial soliloquies in the play. He says that he has no personal reason to kill Caesar. He says he must kill Caesar for the good of Rome and for the people.

Until now, Caesar has not seemed dangerous. He has been as noble as any other man. Brutus is afraid that after Caesar is crowned, his character will change. Brutus believes that power will corrupt Caesar and make him a tyrant.

BRUTUS   **But 'tis common proof**
That lowliness is young ambition's ladder,
Where to the climber upward turns his face.
But when he once attains the upmost round,
He then unto the ladder turns his back,
Looks in the clouds, scorning the base
degrees
By which he did ascend. So Caesar may.

Brutus says that everyone knows that an ambitious man behaves with humility to get to higher places. When he reaches the top, he ignores his supporters and tries to become even more powerful. Once he achieves power, Brutus is afraid that Caesar may behave like this and look down upon all the people who helped him achieve power.

BRUTUS   **And therefore think him as a serpent's egg—**
Which, hatched, would as his kind grow
mischievous—
And kill him in the shell.

Brutus finally decides to join the conspiracy to assassinate Caesar. He says they must think of him as a serpent's egg. If allowed to hatch, the serpent will bring danger to the world. To stop him, they must kill Caesar before it is too late. Brutus has to convince himself to kill Caesar before he has the chance to achieve his ambition.

Lucius re-enters and gives Brutus a letter that has been thrown into his window.

Brutus reads the letter. When he reads the words in the letter "Shall Rome stand under one man's awe?" Brutus wonders if he is being asked to act to save Rome from the tyranny of Caesar's rule.

Brutus makes a promise that he will act to save Rome from the injustice of Caesar's rule.

The conspirators — Cassius, Casca, Decius, Cinna, Metellus Cimber, and Trebonius — now come to meet Brutus. Brutus is introduced to the conspirators.

BRUTUS **No, not an oath. If not the face of men,**
The sufferance of our souls, the time's abuse—
If they be motives weak, break off betimes,
And every man hence to his idle bed.

Cassius proposes that they all seal their participation with an oath, but Brutus disagrees. He uses negative persuasion or reverse psychology to convince the conspirators. He says if the sad faces of our fellow men, the suffering of our own souls and the corruption in Rome are not enough to motivate us, then we should break off the conspiracy and return home. If we are honest, honorable men, we do not need an oath or bond to bind us to our plan.

Brutus insists that an oath is unnecessary. He tells them that they are strong, noble Romans. This way, Brutus inspires the conspirators and establishes himself as their leader.

CASSIUS   **But what of Cicero? Shall we sound him?**
                   I think he will stand very strong with us.

When Cassius asks if they should invite Cicero to join the conspiracy, Brutus disagrees. He knows that Cicero has an independent mind and will not easily follow others orders. He persuades the conspirators to leave Cicero out of the conspiracy.

CASSIUS   **I think it is not meet**
                   Mark Antony, so well beloved of Caesar,
                   Should outlive Caesar.

Cassius suggests that Mark Antony should be killed along with Caesar because Mark Antony would be a dangerous enemy and would turn against them.

BRUTUS   **Our course will seem too bloody, Caius**
                   Cassius,
                   To cut the head off and then hack the limbs,
                   Like wrath in death and envy afterwards,
                   For Antony is but a limb of Caesar.

Brutus disagrees and says that if they killed both Caesar and Mark Antony, their conspiracy would seem too bloody.

Brutus does not want to murder for the sake of killing. He even regrets that Caesar's blood must be spilled. Brutus tells the conspirators that they should be sacrificers, rather than butchers.

He says that after killing Caesar they should appear to be disgusted by what they had to do. This will make it look like their actions were not vengeful.

BRUTUS   **And for Mark Antony, think not of him,**
                    For he can do no more than Caesar's arm
                    When Caesar's head is off.

Brutus reassures the conspirators that they should not worry about Mark Antony because he will be powerless once Caesar is dead.

CASSIUS   **But it is doubtful yet**
                    Whether Caesar will come forth today or no,
                    For he is superstitious grown of late,
                    Quite from the main opinion he held once
                    Of fantasy, of dreams and ceremonies.

Cassius is still doubtful about whether Caesar will go to the Capitol that day. He says Caesar has become superstitious of late. He thinks Caesar might believe the unusual omens of the night and stay away from the Capitol.

Decius Brutus then assures them that he will convince Caesar to come to the Capitol that morning. They decide to commit the murder by the eighth hour.

It is clear that the conspirators are up to no good, yet they attempt to lend credibility to what they do by highlighting their noble Roman ancestry — their blood — in order to spill Caesar's blood. By this bloodletting, they believe they will regain the masculinity and strength that the state has lost. By penetrating Caesar's body, by exposing his weakness, Romans will be men again.

When the conspirators have left, Brutus notices that his servant, Lucius, has fallen asleep.

Portia, Brutus' wife, enters the orchard.

She is disturbed by her husband's strange behavior. She pleads with Brutus and begs him to tell her what is troubling him.

Brutus tries to convince his wife that he is unwell and asks her to return to her bed.

PORTIA **No, my Brutus.**
You have some sick offence within your
mind,
Which by right and virtue of my place
I ought to know of.

Portia is not convinced when Brutus says he is unwell. She says it is not a physical sickness that Brutus is suffering from, but a sickness in his mind. She says, as his wife, she deserves to know what is troubling Brutus. Portia asks her husband why six or seven men visited him that night, with their faces hidden even in the darkness.

BRUTUS   You are my true and honorable wife,
                  As dear to me as are the ruddy drops
                  That visit my sad heart.

Portia tells Brutus that as his wife and because they are married, she has a right to know her husband's secrets. Brutus reminds her that she is his honorable wife who is as precious to him as the blood that flows in his troubled heart.

PORTIA   I grant I am a woman, but withal
                  A woman that Lord Brutus took to wife.
                  I grant I am a woman, but withal
                  A woman well-reputed, Cato's daughter.
                  Think you I am no stronger than my sex,
                  Being so feathered and so husbanded?
                  Tell me your counsels. I will not disclose 'em.

Portia insists that she is a strong woman. She says she is a woman who Lord Brutus chose as his wife. She believes she is worthy because she is the daughter of Cato. She asks if Brutus thinks she is as weak as any other woman. Portia asks Brutus to share his secrets and troubles with her.

PORTIA   I have made strong proof of my constancy,
                  Giving myself a voluntary wound
                  Here in the thigh. Can I bear that with
                  patience, And not my husband's secrets?

Portia further says that she has proven her strength and worthiness by giving herself a wound in the thigh. She tells Brutus that if she is strong enough to bear the pain of a self-inflicted wound, then she is brave enough to keep her husband's secrets.

Brutus is very impressed by Portia's speech, and promises to tell her what has been troubling him.

Portia leaves.

Lucius brings in Caius Ligarius, another conspirator, who has been sick.

LIGARIUS **Soul of Rome,**
Brave son, derived from honorable loins,
Thou like an exorcist hast conjured up
My mortified spirit.

Ligarius is impressed by Brutus' noble character. He says Brutus has reawakened his spirit. He tells Brutus that he will forget his sickness if there is some honorable task that he has to participate in. Ligarius promises his support to the conspiracy and says he will follow Brutus.

They set out for the Capitol together.

SCENE 2

The scene is set in Caesar's house during a night of thunder and lightning.

CAESAR   Nor heaven nor earth have b en at peace
tonight.
Thrice hath Calpurnia in her sleep cried out,
"Help, ho, they murder Caesar!"—Who's
within?

Caesar is commenting on the strange and stormy weather. He says that Calpurnia had dreamt of his murder. Caesar has become superstitious and this characteristic is seen when he sends a servant to instruct his priests to perform a sacrifice.

CALPURNIA   What mean you, Caesar? Think you to
walk forth?
You shall not stir out of your house
today.

Calpurnia enters and pleads with Caesar not to leave home for the day.

Calpurnia, in comparison to noble Portia, is not so well-husbanded, for here Caesar shows himself as weak, superstitious and susceptible to flattery. Yet, there is truth in Calpurnia's dreams and real caring for her husband in her attempts to keep him from going to the Capitol.

CAESAR   Caesar shall forth. The things that threatened
               me Ne'er looked but on my back. When they
               shall see
               The face of Caesar, they are vanished.

Caesar dismisses Calpurnia's plea and insists that he will go out
on that day. He seems to show that he is invincible when he says
that any threats to him vanish when they look upon his face.
Caesar means that he is not afraid of anything that threatens him.
Here, Caesar attempts to show some signs of masculinity in his
response to Calpurnia's account of her dream.

CALPURNIA   Caesar, I never stood on ceremonies,
                  Yet now they fright me. There is one
                  within,
                  Besides the things that we have heard
                  and seen,
                  Recounts most horrid sights seen by
                  the watch.
                  A lioness hath whelped in the streets,
                  And graves have yawned and yielded
                  up their dead.

Calpurnia says she has never believed in his omens. She tells
Caesar that she is frightened by the sights that have been reported
the previous night by the night watchmen. She says the watchmen
had seen a lioness give birth in the streets and the graves cracked
open to let out the dead.

She also says that the night watchmen had seen fierce, fiery
warriors fighting in the clouds until the clouds rained blood onto
the Capitol.

Caesar tells Calpurnia that nobody can change what is fated by the gods. He says that he will go out because the bad omens don't pertain only to him, but also to the world.

CAESAR   **Cowards die many times before their deaths.**
                    The valiant never taste of death but once.

When Calpurnia tells Caesar that the heavens announce the deaths of important people, not commoners, Caesar says that only cowards fear death and the strong people realize that death cannot be avoided and must come to every man.

The servant returns and tells Caesar that the priests advise that he must stay at home today. Caesar rejects the priests' advice. He says the people will think he is a coward if he stayed at home.

CAESAR   **Danger knows full well**
                    That Caesar is more dangerous than he.
                    We are two lions littered in one day,
                    And I the elder and more terrible.

Caesar draws a comparison between himself and Danger, saying that they were both lions born in the same litter, on the same day. Caesar says he is the older and more dangerous of the two lions. He seems overconfident and implies that nothing dangerous can happen to him.

However, Calpurnia does finally convince Caesar to stay at home. She says he must send a message to Antony, who will tell the senators that Caesar is unwell. As Calpurnia kneels before him, Caesar is persuaded. Here, the reader is meant to remember

Portia's actions in the previous scene. She, too, knelt before her husband and Brutus was persuaded. Shakespeare invites the readers to draw comparisons between the two and see a strong woman married to a strong man and a weak woman married to a weak man.

Decius enters and Caesar decides to send the message with him.

CAESAR   **Shall Caesar send a lie?**
Have I in conquest stretched mine arm so far
To be afraid to tell greybeards the truth?
Decius, go tell them Caesar will not come.

Decius asks Caesar what reason he must give to the senators for Caesar's absence. Caesar refuses to tell a lie that he his unwell. He tells Decius to tell the senators simply that he will not come. In this scene, we see that Caesar seems unable to give one command and follow it through, but is constantly changing his mind.

CAESAR   **Calpurnia here, my wife, stays me at home.**
She dreamt tonight she saw my statue,
Which, like a fountain with an hundred
spouts, Did run pure blood. And many lusty
Romans
Came smiling and did bathe their hands in it.

Caesar confesses to Decius that he is staying at home at Calpurnia's insistence. He tells Decius about Calpurnia's ominous dream in which she saw a statue of him, flowing with blood.

Decius now begins to flatter Caesar, knowing that Caesar will change his mind if he is praised and made to feel important.

Decius says that Calpurnia's dream is wrongly interpreted. He says the vision of blood flowing from Caesar's statue is a symbol of Caesar reviving Rome. The vision of smiling Romans bathing their hands in the blood shows that they are drawing strength and vitality from mighty Caesar.

DECIUS   And know it now: the senate have concluded
To give this day a crown to mighty Caesar.

Decius cleverly adds that the Senate has decided to crown Caesar that day, knowing that Caesar will find it difficult to resist the temptation of a crown. In an attempt to make Caesar aware of his masculinity, Decius says that the Senate will ridicule Caesar for being weak and frightened by his wife's dreams.

Caesar then says he is ashamed that he believed Calpurnia's foolish fears. He declares that he will go to the Capitol.

Publius and the remaining conspirators — all except Cassius — enter.

Brutus informs Caesar that it is after eight o'clock. Caesar warmly welcomes Antony and prepares to leave for the Capitol.

SCENE 3

Artemidorus enters a street near the Capitol reading from a paper. It is a letter he has written, that warns Caesar of danger. In his letter, Artemidorus mentions the names of all the conspirators.

ARTEMIDORUS **Here I will stand till Caesar pass along,**
And as a suitor will I give him this.
My heart laments that virtue cannot
live Out of the teeth of emulation.
If thou read this, O Caesar, thou mayst
live.
If not, the Fates with traitors do
contrive.

Artemidorus plans to give the letter to Caesar as though it was a petition. He says that Caesar may survive if he reads his letter.

This brief scene allows the reader to see another opinion of Caesar. Artemidorus is a Roman who loves Caesar and sees the conspirators as traitors. From Artemidorus' viewpoint, the reader gets a hint of the greatness that was once Caesar.

Given that Artemidorus knows all about the conspirators and their plans, it is made clear that the they have not kept quiet. Caesar is among the few who do not know what is about to happen.

SCENE 4

Portia and Lucius are standing on the street in front of Brutus' house. Portia is extremely worried about Brutus.

PORTIA   **Yes, bring me word, boy, if thy lord look well,**
For he went sickly forth.

Portia commands her servant, Lucius to hurry to the Capitol. She asks him to see if Brutus looks well because he looked uneasy and sick when he left. Portia is anxious and reacts violently to noises that she imagines she can hear. She thinks these sounds come from the Capitol.

A soothsayer enters and says that he is on his way to see Caesar as he approaches the Capitol.

Portia asks the soothsayer if he knows about any plans to harm Caesar. The soothsayer says he only fears what may happen to Caesar.

SOOTHSAYER   **I'll get to a place more void, and there**
Speak to great Caesar as he comes
along.

The soothsayer leaves to find a place from where he can speak to Caesar as he passes on the way to the Capitol.

PORTIA   Run, Lucius, and commend me to my lord.
              Say I am merry. Come to me again,
              And bring me word what he doth say to thee.

Portia sends Lucius to tell Brutus that she is happy. She tells him to then report back immediately to her.

ACT THREE

SCENE 1

Caesar approaches the Capitol with Antony, Lepidus, and all the conspirators.

CAESAR   (to the soothsayer)
             The ides of March are come.

Caesar sees the soothsayer and reminds the man that it was the ides of March. The soothsayer replies that the day is not yet over.

ARTEMIDORUS   **O Caesar, read mine first, for mine's a suit That touches Caesar nearer. Read it, great Caesar.**

Artemidorus calls to Caesar, urging him to read the paper containing his warning, but Caesar refuses to read it. He says he will read whatever concerns himself last. Here, Caesar seems to be giving more importance to the people's petitions and requests, rather than to any that involve him.

Caesar enters the Capitol.

POPILIUS LENA (to Cassius)
I wish your enterprise today may
thrive.

Popilius Lena whispers these words to Cassius. Cassius tells Brutus that he is afraid that their plan has been discovered. Brutus reassures Cassius that Popilius Lena was not referring to the conspiracy.

The other senators enter the Capitol, and Trebonius deliberately takes Antony away so that he will not interfere with the assassination.

CAESAR   I must prevent thee, Cimber.
These crouching and these lowly courtesies
Might fire the blood of ordinary men
And turn preordinance and first decree
Into the law of children. Be not fond,
To think that Caesar bears such rebel blood
That will be thawed from the true quality
With that which melteth fools—I mean, sweet words,
Low crookèd curtsies, and base spaniel fawning.

When Metellus Cimber kneels before Caesar to request him to allow his brother Publius Cimber to return to Rome as a citizen, Caesar refuses. He tells Metellus that flattery might please other men and make a mockery of the law. Caesar says he will not be affected by such flattery. Caesar tells Metellus that he will not be flattered by low bows and fawning. He refuses to allow Metellus' brother to return just because he is flattered by Metellus' behavior.

Brutus, Casca, and the others also plead along with Metellus Cimber.

The conspirators ritualistically circle their prey—Caesar—and mock him with their courtesies. The act of Metellus Cimber kneeling before Caesar is essentially a trick by the conspirators to allow them to get close enough to Caesar to kill him, and to keep others, who may come to his aid, away.

CAESAR   **I could be well moved if I were as you.**
If I could pray to move, prayers would move
me.
But I am constant as the northern star,
Of whose true-fixed and resting quality
There is no fellow in the firmament.

When Cassius kneels to plead for the return of Publius Cimber, Caesar still refuses and compares himself to the North Star in the sky. He says that if he could beg others to change their minds, then he could also be convinced by pleas. Caesar says he is as immovable as the North Star which has no equal in the sky. Here, he is portrayed as self-important and vain. He continues to say that he banished Publius Cimber for a reason and he will not change his mind.

CASCA   Speak, hands, for me!

Suddenly, Casca stabs Caesar from behind. The other conspirators also stab Caesar. Brutus stabs him last.

CAESAR   *Et tu, Bruté?* —Then fall, Caesar.

Caesar expresses shock at Brutus' treachery. He falls at the feet of Pompey's statue and dies.

While chaos erupts and citizens and senators are trying to escape the Capitol, Brutus attempts to calm them by saying that only Caesar had to die for being ambitious.

Trebonius arrives to tell the conspirators that Mark Antony has fled to his house in shock. He says that men, women and children are crying and running in the streets as though it were doomsday.

BRUTUS   Stoop, Romans, stoop,
            And let us bathe our hands in Caesar's blood
            Up to the elbows, and besmear our swords.
            Then walk we forth, even to the marketplace,
            And waving our red weapons o'er our heads
            Let's all cry, "Peace, freedom, and liberty!"

Brutus encourages the other conspirators to dip their hands and swords in Caesar's blood and walk outside, proclaiming peace, freedom, and liberty.

ANTONY'S SERVANT   If Brutus will vouchsafe that Antony
May safely come to him and be resolved
How Caesar hath deserved to lie in death,
Mark Antony shall not love Caesar dead
So well as Brutus living, but will follow
The fortunes and affairs of noble Brutus
Thorough the hazards of this untrod state
With all true faith. So says my master Antony.

A servant comes to Brutus with a request from Mark Antony. Antony asks if he will be allowed to come to them and see Caesar's body. He asks if Brutus will explain his reasons for committing the murder. Antony promises to pledge his loyalty to Brutus.

Brutus agrees to meet Mark Antony and calls him a wise and honorable Roman. Brutus promises that Antony will not be harmed if he comes to see him.

ANTONY   No place will please me so, no means of death,
As here by Caesar, and by you cut off,
The choice and master spirits of this age.

Antony enters.

He asks the conspirators if they were going to kill him too. He volunteers to die in the same place where noble Caesar died.

Mark Antony is able to expertly mask his true feelings, not only so that he can place himself in a position to avenge Caesar's death, but also so that he can find his own position of power. In contrast to the conspirators—even the sharpest of them, Cassius—Antony is strong and politically savvy. Gone are the images of him as womanizer and drunkard. He has taken charge at the moment of greatest danger and he does so by manipulating Brutus' naïve sense of honor.

BRUTUS   O Antony, beg not your death of us.
Though now we must appear bloody and
cruel
As by our hands and this our present act
You see we do—yet see you but our hands
And this the bleeding business they have
done.
Our hearts you see not. They are pitiful.
And pity to the general wrong of Rome—
As fire drives out fire, so pity pity—
Hath done this deed on Caesar.

Brutus tells Antony not to beg the conspirators to kill him. Brutus insists that Antony has only seen their hands covered in the blood of Caesar. Their bloody hands are a symbol of their crime. He says Antony has not seen their hearts. Brutus tells Antony that their hearts are filled with pity for Caesar, but they had to kill him for the good of Rome. Brutus continues to say that the conspirators' swords are too blunt to harm Antony. Their hearts are only filled with love and respect for him.

BRUTUS   Only be patient till we have appeased
The multitude, beside themselves with fear,
And then we will deliver to you the cause,
Why I, that did love Caesar when I struck
him,
Have thus proceeded.

Brutus promises Antony that as soon as they have calmed the people of Rome, he will tell Antony why he killed Caesar, even though he loved him.

ANTONY —That I did love thee, Caesar, O, 'tis true.
If then thy spirit look upon us now,
Shall it not grieve thee dearer than thy death
To see thy Antony making his peace,
Shaking the bloody fingers of thy foes—

Antony pretends to be friendly with the conspirators and shakes their hands. He begs Caesar's forgiveness and says that he truly loved him. If Caesar's spirit was watching them, Antony says it would hurt Caesar more than death to see Antony making peace with his murderers in front of his dead body.

ANTONY That's all I seek,
And am moreover suitor that I may
Produce his body to the marketplace,
And in the pulpit, as becomes a friend,
Speak in the order of his funeral.

Antony requests permission to make a speech at Caesar's funeral. Brutus agrees to his request and allows him to make a speech at Caesar's funeral.

CASSIUS (aside to Brutus)
You know not what you do.
Do not consent
That Antony speak at his funeral.
Know you how much the people may be moved
By that which he will utter?

Cassius is hesitant to allow Mark Antony to speak at Caesar's funeral because he thinks the people will be influenced by

Antony's words to turn against the conspirators. Brutus assures Cassius that he will speak before Antony and explain to the people why they killed Caesar.

ANTONY **O, pardon me, thou bleeding piece of earth,**
That I am meek and gentle with these
butchers!
Thou art the ruins of the noblest man
That ever lived in the tide of times.

When the conspirators have left, Antony begs forgiveness from Caesar's dead body. He asks for forgiveness because he was polite and gentle with the conspirators who he calls "butchers". He praises Caesar and says he was the most noble man to have lived on earth.

ANTONY **And Caesar's spirit, ranging for revenge,**
With Ate by his side come hot from hell,
Shall in these confines with a monarch's voice
Cry "Havoc!" and let slip the dogs of war,
That this foul deed shall smell above the
earth
With carrion men, groaning for burial.

Antony predicts that Caesar's death will result in war and chaos across Italy. He says Caesar, longing for revenge will bring war upon the land. The earth will be covered in the dead bodies of men waiting to be buried. Here, Antony vows to seek revenge on Brutus and the other conspirators by starting a civil war.

A servant enters and tells Antony that Octavius Caesar is seven leagues away from Rome. Julius Caesar had written to Octavius and called him to Rome.

ANTONY Post back with speed and tell him what hath chanced.
Here is a mourning Rome, a dangerous Rome,
No Rome of safety for Octavius yet.
Hie hence, and tell him so. —Yet, stay awhile.
Thou shalt not back till I have borne this corse
Into the marketplace. There shall I try,
In my oration, how the people take
The cruèl issue of these bloody men.
According to the which, thou shalt discourse
To young Octavius of the state of things.
Lend me your hand.

Antony tells Octavius' servant to tell Octavius what has happened. He says Octavius is coming to a country that is now in mourning for Caesar. It is a dangerous Rome, and is not safe for Octavius.

He says that he is going to the marketplace to give a speech at Caesar's funeral. When he gives his speech, Antony will be able to understand how the people react to the evil deed committed by the conspirators. He tells Octavius' servant to wait until he gives his speech and then report to his master about how the crowds reacted. *The two men exit, carrying the body of Caesar.*

SCENE 2

The plebeians crowd the Forum, demanding answers about Caesar's death.

PLEBEIANS   **We will be satisfied! Let us be satisfied!**

Brutus and Cassius enter the Forum, which is filled with citizens demanding answers.

BRUTUS   **Then follow me and give me audience, friends.**
—Cassius, go you into the other street
And part the numbers.
—Those that will hear me speak, let 'em stay here.
Those that will follow Cassius, go with him,
And public reasons shall be rendered
Of Caesar's death.

 They divide the crowd. Some of the people go with Cassius to hear his argument while Brutus speaks to the citizens who remain behind at the Forum.

BRUTUS   If there be any in this assembly, any dear friend of Caesar's, to him I say that Brutus' love to Caesar was no less than his. If then that friend demand why Brutus rose against Caesar, this is my answer: not that I loved Caesar less, but that I loved Rome more.

Brutus asks the citizens to remain quiet until he finishes his speech. He asks them to remember that he is an honorable man. Brutus tells the crowd to think carefully before they judge him. He insists that he too loved Caesar and says he did not kill him because he did not like Caesar, but because he loved Rome more.

BRUTUS   Had you rather Caesar were living and die all slaves, than that Caesar were dead, to live all free men? As Caesar loved me, I weep for him. As he was fortunate, I rejoice at it. As he was valiant, I honor him. But as he was ambitious, I slew him.

Brutus asks the crowd if they would prefer to live in a world where Caesar was living and die as slaves or if they would rather live as free men. Brutus says that since Caesar was good to him and treated him well, he weeps for him. Brutus says that he rejoiced in Caesar's triumphs and victories. But Brutus says Caesar's ambition was the reason why he killed him.

Brutus goes on to ask the people in the crowd if there was anyone there who would prefer to live life as a slave. He questions the identity of the people and asks if there was anyone in the crowd who wasn't a Roman. He also asks the people in the crowd if they loved their country. Brutus says that by killing Caesar, he has offended anyone in the crowd who would have preferred to live as a slave, anyone who was not a Roman, or anyone who did not love his country.

Here, Brutus questions the people's loyalty to Rome and asks if they were truly patriotic citizens of Rome.

The citizens are convinced and at the end of Brutus' speech, they cheer him. Before Brutus leaves, he asks the people to listen to Antony's funeral speech. He tells them that he should be allowed to leave alone. Brutus tells the people to stay with Antony and pay their respects to Caesar.

ANTONY   **Friends, Romans, countrymen, lend me your ears. I come to bury Caesar, not to praise him.**
The evil that men do lives after them;
The good is oft interrèd with their bones.
So let it be with Caesar. The noble Brutus
Hath told you Caesar was ambitious.
If it were so, it was a grievous fault,
And grievously hath Caesar answered it.
Here, under leave of Brutus and the rest—
For Brutus is an honorable man;
So are they all, all honorable men—
Come I to speak in Caesar's funeral.

Antony draws the crowd and calls them "friends, Romans, countrymen" as he begins his speech. By emphasizing the word "friends" first, he refers to the people as his companions. He calls them "Romans" second and "countrymen" third, showing that they were friends first before countrymen. This makes the relationship between Antony and the people more personal.

He says he has come to bury Caesar and not to praise him. He reminds the people in the crowd that the evil that men do while they live, lives on after their death; whereas their good deeds are often forgotten. By declaring Caesar a good man, Antony successfully turns his audience's attention from the "evil ambition" of which Brutus spoke.

Antony tells the people that noble Brutus told them that Caesar was ambitious and was therefore killed. He agrees that if Caesar was ambitious, it was a great fault in his character. If it was true, then Caesar paid the price for being ambitious.

Antony goes on to say that he has come to speak at the funeral with permission from Brutus, who was a noble man. He repeatedly calls Brutus, and the other conspirators noble men, as though to mock their nobility. By repeatedly saying that Brutus was noble, Antony indirectly plays on the emotions of the people. He wants them to actually question whether Brutus and the conspirators were really noble in their actions.

Antony says Caesar was his friend, who was faithful and fair to him. Antony repeats that noble Brutus said that Caesar was ambitious. He seems to ask the people, surely noble Brutus cannot be wrong, can he? He reminds the people of Caesar, who brought many captives to Rome and brought wealth to the city with their ransoms.

ANTONY   Did this in Caesar seem ambitious?
          When the poor have cried, Caesar hath wept.
          Ambition should be made of sterner stuff.
          Yet Brutus says he was ambitious,
          And Brutus is an honorable man.

Antony asks if Caesar's act of bringing wealth to the city, for the people, was the work of an ambitious man. He says when the poor cried, so did Caesar. Antony tells the people that if he was truly ambitious, Caesar would not have been so concerned for the welfare of the people. Still, Brutus says Caesar was ambitious. Antony tells the people to ask themselves if Brutus was right in saying Caesar was ambitious.

ANTONY   You all did see that on the Lupercal
          I thrice presented him a kingly crown,
          Which he did thrice refuse. Was this
          ambition?
          Yet Brutus says he was ambitious,
          And, sure, he is an honorable man.

Antony reminds the people of the feast of Lupercal, when he offered Caesar a crown three times. He asks the people if it shows that Caesar was ambitious, if he refused to accept the crown thrice. Despite all this, Antony says, Brutus called Caesar ambitious.

Although Antony says that he does not want to disagree with what Brutus has told the people, he has won the support of the crowd. He has made them understand that Brutus was wrong to think that Caesar was ambitious.

ANTONY   O masters, if I were disposed to stir
              Your hearts and minds to mutiny and rage,
              I should do Brutus wrong, and Cassius
              wrong— Who, you all know, are honorable
              men.

Antony tells the people that he does not want to make them rise up in mutiny against Caesar's murderers. He says that he did not want to anger them and make them take revenge on the conspirators. If he did this, he says he would offend Brutus and Cassius.

However, it is clear that Antony is indirectly trying to make the people rebel.

ANTONY   But here's a parchment with the seal of
              Caesar.
              I found it in his closet. 'Tis his will.
              Let but the commons here this testament—
              Which, pardon me, I do not mean to read—
              And they would go and kiss dead Caesar's
              wounds
              And dip their napkins in his sacred blood,
              Yea, beg s hair of him for memory,
              And, dying, mention it within their wills,
              Bequeathing it as a rich legacy
              Unto their issue.

Antony shows the people a parchment that he says is the will of Caesar, which he found in his room. He says the people would know the true worth of Caesar if they could hear what was written in the will. Antony tells them he will not read the will. He says if the people knew what was written in Caesar's will, they would kiss his wounds in reverence. They would dip their handkerchiefs in his blood and beg for a lock of his hair to cherish as a memory of Caesar. Antony says that the people would bequeath the lock of Caesar's hair in their own wills as a priceless legacy.

FOURTH PLEBEIAN   **We'll hear the will. Read it,**
                                 Mark Antony!

The people in the crowd shout and demand to hear Caesar's will.

ANTONY   **Will you be patient? Will you stay awhile?**
                   I have o'ershot myself to tell you of it.
                   I fear I wrong the honorable men
                   Whose daggers have stabbed Caesar. I do
                   fear it.

Antony asks the crowd to be patient and calm. He says that he might have made a mistake by telling them about Caesar's will. He says by mentioning Caesar's will, he may have angered the conspirators who stabbed Caesar. He is cleverly playing on the people's emotions. By reminding the people of the conspirators' brutal act, Antony is turning the people against Brutus and the conspirators.

FOURTH PLEBEIAN   **They were traitors! "Honorable**
                                 men"!

The crowd of people becomes restless, shouting for revenge against the conspirators, who they call traitors. They swear to take revenge on the conspirators when they are shown Caesar's bleeding corpse and told of how ungrateful Brutus stabbed Caesar.

ANTONY   **Through this the well-beloved Brutus**
                stabbed. And as he plucked his cursèd steel
                away,
                Mark how the blood of Caesar followed it,
                As rushing out of doors, to be resolved
                If Brutus so unkindly knocked, or no.
                For Brutus, as you know, was Caesar's angel.
                Judge, O you gods, how dearly Caesar loved
                him!
                This was the most unkindest cut of all.

Antony shows the people each stab wound on Caesar's lifeless body and tells them where each conspirator stabbed Caesar. He shows them where Brutus had stabbed Caesar and says as Brutus removed his dagger, the blood followed it and flowed from Caesar's body. Antony tells them that Caesar's blood seemed to flow as though it was rushing out of a door to see if it was really Brutus who had knocked so rudely. He reminds the people that Caesar loved Brutus. Antony describes Brutus' act of stabbing Caesar as the "unkindest cut of all".

Antony tells the people that Caesar was so shocked by Brutus' betrayal that his heart burst and he fell at the feet of Pompey's statue while the blood dripped from his cloak. Antony tells them that as Caesar fell, so did all the men of Rome because they had allowed traitors to triumph.

When Antony lifts Caesar's cloak and the people see his body, they vow to kill the traitors and burn their houses.

ANTONY Good friends, sweet friends! Let me not stir
you up
To such a sudden flood of mutiny.
They that have done this deed are honorable.
What private griefs they have, alas, I know
not,
That made them do it. They are wise and
honorable,
And will no doubt, with reasons answer you.
I come not, friends, to steal away your hearts.
I am no orator, as Brutus is,
But, as you know me all, a plain blunt man
That love my friend.

Antony tells the people that he does not want to make them rise
up in mutiny. He says the people who have killed Caesar are
honorable men. He says he does not know what personal grudges
they had against Caesar that made them kill him. Antony tells the
crowd that the conspirators will surely give them a reason for
their actions. He says that he has not come to steal the people's
loyalty. Antony reminds them that he is not a skilled orator like
Brutus, but he is just a plain man who loved his friend.

ANTONY Here is the will, and under Caesar's seal
To every Roman citizen he gives—
To every several man—seventy-five
drachmas.

The people promise to take revenge and burn Brutus' house.
Antony then reminds the people of Caesar's will and asks them if
they know what Caesar has done to deserve their love.

When they hear that Caesar has left money and property to the Roman people, they realize Caesar's generosity.

The mob leaves to cremate Caesar's body with due respect and honor, and promise to burn the houses of the conspirators and to wreak destruction in the city.

ANTONY   **Mischief, thou art afoot,**
Take thou what course thou wilt!

Antony is now satisfied that he has sown the seeds of trouble and says to himself that this trouble will take its own course.

OCTAVIUS' SERVANT   **I have heard him say, Brutus**
and Cassius
Are rid like madmen through
the gates of Rome.

A servant enters and tells Antony that Octavius has arrived in Rome and is waiting with Lepidus at Caesar's house. Antony is pleased and says he will visit him immediately. The servant also tells Antony that Brutus and Cassius have fled Rome. Antony thinks that they may have heard of how he had convinced the people to take revenge.

SCENE 3

An angry mob roams the streets of Rome.

Cinna the poet is on his way to attend Caesar's funeral when he is caught by the angry mob. They demand to know who he is and where he is going. He tells them that his name is Cinna and that he is on his way to attend Caesar's funeral.

FIRST PLEBEIAN   **Tear him to pieces. He's a conspirator.**

When the people hear that he is Cinna, they assume that he is one of the conspirators. They begin to assault him.

CINNA THE POET   **I am Cinna the poet. I am Cinna the poet.**

He pleads that he is Cinna the poet and not Cinna the conspirator. The rebels reply that they will kill him anyway because of his bad poetry.

The people do not care if they have the wrong Cinna. They believe that someone must pay for the crime. They drag Cinna the poet away and the crowd leaves, declaring that they intend to burn the houses of Brutus, Cassius, Decius, Casca, and Caius Ligarius.

ACT FOUR

SCENE 1

Antony meets with Octavius and Lepidus to discuss how they can shift the balance of power in Rome in their favor.

ANTONY **These many, then, shall die. Their names are pricked.**

Antony meets with Octavius and Lepidus. They make a list to decide who should be murdered so that they can reclaim power in Rome.

OCTAVIUS (to Lepidus)
 Your brother too must die. Consent you, Lepidus?

They have a long list, on which the names of Lepidus' own brother, Antony's nephew, and many of Rome's senators are mentioned.

ANTONY　This is a slight, unmeritable man,
　　　　　　Meet to be sent on errands. Is it fit,
　　　　　　The threefold world divided, he should stand
　　　　　　One of the three to share it?

Antony sends Lepidus on an errand to fetch Caesar's will from his house. When he leaves, Antony and Octavius discuss whether Lepidus will be a suitable choice as a member of the triumvirate.

ANTONY　And though we lay these honors on this man
　　　　　　To ease ourselves of divers slanderous loads,
　　　　　　He shall but bear them as the ass bears gold,
　　　　　　To groan and sweat under the business,
　　　　　　Either led or driven, as we point the way.

Antony says that if they give Lepidus a role in the triumvirate and make him a ruler, he will perform his duties like a horse that carries gold. He will groan and sweat under the burden of responsibility. Antony says Lepidus will do only what he is directed to do by them. Here, Antony seems to ask if Lepidus has any real leadership qualities.

Octavius does not want to argue with Antony but says that Lepidus is an honorable, brave soldier.

ANTONY　　　And now, Octavius,
Listen great things. Brutus and
Cassius
Are levying powers. We must straight
make head.
Therefore let our alliance be combined,
Our best friends made, our means
stretched.
And let us presently go sit in council
How covert matters may be best
disclosed,
And open perils surest answered.

Antony then tells Octavius that they have more important matters to discuss. He says that Brutus and Cassius are forming armies to go to war. Antony tells Octavius that they must make plans so that they can find out Brutus and Cassius' secrets and find a way to confront them.

OCTAVIUS　　　Let us do so. For we are at stake
And bayed about with many enemies.
And some that smile have in their
hearts, I fear,
Millions of mischiefs.

Antony and Octavius agree to form an alliance and combat Brutus and Cassius' armies. Octavius says that they were in danger and surrounded by enemies. He says he is afraid that even those who smile at them are plotting against them.

SCENE 2

Outside of his tent at a camp near Sardis, Brutus welcomes Titinius and Pindarus. They come to tell him that Cassius is approaching.

BRUTUS —Your master, Pindarus,
In his own change or by ill officers
Hath given me some worthy cause to wish
Things done, undone. But if he be at hand
I shall be satisfied.

Brutus complains to Pindarus and says that Cassius has offended him. He says he is waiting to hear and explanation from Cassius. Pindarus, Cassius' servant, assures Brutus that his master will give him a satisfactory explanation.

LUCILIUS With courtesy and with respect enough.
But not with such familiar instances
Nor with such free and friendly conferences
As he hath used of old.

Brutus asks Lucilius how Cassius treated him. Lucilius says that Cassius was courteous and respectful. However, he says that Cassius was not as friendly as he used to be earlier.

BRUTUS   Thou hast described
A hot friend cooling. Ever note, Lucilius,
When love begins to sicken and decay,
It useth enforcèd ceremony.
There are no tricks in plain and simple faith.
But hollow men, like horses hot at hand,
Make gallant show and promise of their
mettle.

Brutus tells Lucilius that when a friend begins to get tired of you, they begin to treat you indifferently. He says insincere men are like horses at the start of a race. They make an enthusiastic show of their spirit. Brutus seems to think that Cassius is insincere in his loyalty.

CASSIUS   Most noble brother, you have done me
wrong.

Cassius arrives with most of his army. He accuses Brutus of having wronged him.

BRUTUS   Judge me, you gods! Wrong I mine enemies?
And if not so, how should I wrong a brother?

Brutus tells Cassius that he would not even mistreat his enemies, and would definitely not insult a friend. Brutus suggests that they speak privately inside his tent so that their armies will not see them arguing.

CASSIUS   Pindarus,
Bid our commanders lead their charges off
A little from this ground.

Cassius and Brutus order their servants to inform their armies to move away so that they can have some privacy while they speak inside Brutus' tent.

SCENE 3

As soon as they are inside Brutus' tent, Cassius accuses Brutus of having wronged him by punishing an officer. Brutus punished Lucius Pella for taking bribes from the people of Sardis, even though Cassius had written letters in his defense.

BRUTUS   **Let me tell you, Cassius, you yourself**
                Are much condemned to have an itching palm,
                To sell and mart your offices for gold
                To undeservers.

Brutus accuses Cassius of giving away important positions in return for money. He goes on to tell Cassius that he avoids punishment for these corrupt actions only because he is respected.

BRUTUS   Remember March, the ides of March remember
Did not great Julius bleed for justice' sake?
What villain touched his body, that did stab,
And not for justice? What, shall one of us
That struck the foremost man of all this world
But for supporting robbers, shall we now
Contaminate our fingers with base bribes,
And sell the mighty space of our large honors
For so much trash as may be graspèd thus?
I had rather be a dog and bay the moon
Than such a Roman.

Brutus reminds Cassius that Julius Caesar died so that they could maintain justice in Rome. Brutus asks Cassius if they had killed the most powerful man in the world so that they could support robbers and take bribes. Brutus says that he would prefer to be a dog that howls at the moon than a dishonorable Roman who accepts money in exchange for a powerful position.

BRUTUS   I did send to you
For certain sums of gold, which you denied
me,
For I can raise no money by vile means.
By heaven, I had rather coin my heart
And drop my blood for drachmas than to
wring
From the hard hands of peasants their vile
trash
By any indirection. I did send
To you for gold to pay my legions,
Which you denied me.

Brutus then reminds Cassius that he had requested some gold from him, which Cassius had refused. Brutus had needed the money to pay his soldiers. Brutus says he cannot raise money by dishonorable methods like taking bribes. He says he would rather turn his heart into money and drops of his blood into coins, than rob money from hardworking people.

CASSIUS   I did not. He was but a fool that brought
My answer back. Brutus hath rived my heart.
A friend should bear his friend's infirmities,
But Brutus makes mine greater than they are.

Cassius denies that he refused to send money to Brutus. He is unhappy that Brutus, his friend no longer loves him. He says a friend must understand another friend's weaknesses but Brutus does not do that. When Brutus says that he does not like Cassius' faults, Cassius goes on to say that if Brutus was a true friend, he would not judge Cassius so harshly.

CASSIUS   There is my dagger,
And here my naked breast. Within, a heart
Dearer than Plutus' mine, richer than gold.
If that thou beest a Roman, take it forth.
I, that denied thee gold, will give my heart.
Strike, as thou didst at Caesar. For, I know
When thou didst hate him worst, thou lovedst
him better
Than ever thou lovedst Cassius.

Cassius tells Brutus to kill him. He offers him his dagger and tells Brutus to stab him in his chest, inside which is his heart. Cassius says his heart is more precious than all the silver in the Underworld. His heart is more valuable than gold. He challenges Brutus and says if he was a true Roman, he would take his heart out. Cassius tells Brutus to strike him like he struck Caesar. Cassius says he knew that even though Brutus disliked Caesar because he was ambitious, Brutus loved Caesar more than he loved him.

BRUTUS   O Cassius, you are yokèd with a lamb
That carries anger as the flint bears fire,
Who, much enforcèd, shows a hasty spark
And straight is cold again.

Brutus tells Cassius to put away his dagger. He dismisses Cassius' insults, saying that it is because Cassius is in a bad mood. Brutus compares himself to a quiet lamb and says his anger is like a flint striking a fire. Like the fire lit from a flint, his anger is brief and is quickly extinguished.

Brutus and Cassius are reconciled and they shake hands in renewed friendship.

BRUTUS   **O Cassius, I am sick of many griefs.**

Brutus tells Cassius that he has had many sorrows recently.

BRUTUS   **No man bears sorrow better. Portia is dead.**

Brutus tells Cassius that his wife Portia is dead.

CASSIUS   **How 'scaped I killing when I crossed you so?**
O insupportable and touching loss!
Upon what sickness?

Cassius is shocked to hear the news of Portia's death. He asks Brutus how he did not kill him after their heated argument. Cassius says Portia's loss is irreplaceable and very sad. He asks Brutus what sickness she died from.

BRUTUS   **Impatient of my absence,**
And grief that young Octavius with Mark
Antony
Have made themselves so strong—for with
her death
That tidings came—with this she fell distract
And, her attendants absent, swallowed fire.

Brutus tells Cassius that Portia was upset by his absence and unhappy to hear that Octavius and Antony had gathered a strong army. Brutus says that the news of Portia's death came at the same time as the news of Antony and Octavius' strong army. He says Portia was full of despair at this news and when her servants were away, she swallowed hot coals.

Brutus and Cassius drink some wine together. They are soon joined by Titinius and Messala.

Brutus tells them that he has received news of Antony and Octavius' powerful army.

MESSALA   **That by proscription and bills of outlawry,**
Octavius, Antony and Lepidus
Have put to death a hundred senators.

Messala tells Brutus and Cassius that Octavius, Antony and Lepidus are marching with their armies to Philippi. He says they have put to death a hundred senators. Messala tells Brutus that Cicero was also killed.

Messala goes on to ask Brutus if he had received any news from his wife, Portia. Brutus knows that she is dead but does not say this. He denies that he has heard from Portia.

MESSALA   **Then like a Roman bear the truth I tell.**
For certain she is dead and by strange
manner.

When Messala repeatedly asks if Brutus has heard any news from Portia, Brutus asks if Messala has heard anything. Messala says he has not, but Brutus tells him to speak truly as a Roman should. Messala then tells Brutus to hear his news with courage like a true Roman.

BRUTUS   Why, farewell, Portia. We must die, Messala.
With meditating that she must die once,
I have the patience to endure it now.

When Messala tells Brutus that Portia is dead, Brutus reacts calmly. Brutus says that it is true that all men must die. He says he knew that Portia must die at some time. He knew that her death was inevitable. Now, Brutus consoles himself and says, that thought will give him the strength to live without her.

BRUTUS   Well, to our work alive. What do you think
Of marching to Philippi presently?

Brutus says that they must march toward Philippi to meet the enemy immediately.

CASSIUS   'Tis better that the enemy seek us.
So shall he waste his means, weary his soldiers,
Doing himself offense, whilst we, lying still,
Are full of rest, defense and nimbleness.

Cassius disagrees. He tells Brutus that it would be better to wait for the enemy to come to them. This way, the enemy forces would be weakened from travel, while their own men will be energetic and ready to battle.

BRUTUS　　The people 'twixt Philippi and this ground
　　　　　　Do stand but in a forced affection,
　　　　　　For they have grudged us contribution.
　　　　　　The enemy, marching along by them,
　　　　　　By them shall make a fuller number up,
　　　　　　Come on refreshed, new-added, and
　　　　　　encouraged,
　　　　　　From which advantage shall we cut him off
　　　　　　If at Philippi we do face him there,
　　　　　　These people at our back.

Brutus tells Cassius that the people who live in the area between Sardis and Philippi are loyal to Brutus and Cassius only because they are forced. He says these people do not support them willingly. Brutus warns Cassius that if they wait for Antony and Octavius to approach, then the people of Sardis will join the enemy's army. If they do that, then Antony and Octavius will have increased the size of their army. They will attack Brutus and Cassius' forces with renewed courage.

Brutus says that they must not give Antony and Octavius an advantage over them.

Brutus goes on to say that they have an opportunity which they should not lose.

When his guests have departed, Brutus tells his servant Lucius to call some of his men to sleep with him in his tent. Varro and Claudius enter and say they will keep watch while Brutus sleeps. However, Brutus tells them to lie down and sleep as well.

Brutus then asks Lucius to play some music while he reads a book. Lucius sings for some time, then falls asleep. Brutus continues to read.

BRUTUS   How ill this taper burns!—Ha, who comes here?
                 I think it is the weakness of mine eyes
                 That shapes this monstrous apparition.
                 It comes upon me.—Art thou any thing?
                 Art thou some god, some angel, or some devil
                 That makest my blood cold and my hair to stare?
                 Speak to me what thou art.

Brutus is suddenly interrupted by the appearance of Caesar's ghost. Brutus asks the ghost if it is some god, some angel, or some devil.

GHOST   Thy evil spirit, Brutus.

The ghost says that it is Brutus' evil spirit.

GHOST   To tell thee thou shalt see me at Philippi.

Brutus then asks why the ghost has appeared. The ghost says it has come to tell Brutus that they will meet again at Philippi.

After the ghost disappears, Brutus calls to Lucius, Varro and Claudius. He asks them why each of them shouted out in their sleep. He then asks if they had seen anything unusual. They all say they that they had not seen or heard anything.

Brutus' dream foreshadows—and Brutus realizes—that he will die in the battles to come, and that his death will not be the last. The events Brutus initiated with the murder of Caesar will continue to result in more death.

ACT FIVE

SCENE 1

Octavius and Antony with their armies await the arrival of Brutus and Cassius with their armies on the fields of Philippi.

OCTAVIUS   Now, Antony, our hopes are answered.
You said the enemy would not come down
But keep the hills and upper regions.
It proves not so. Their battles are at hand.
They mean to warn us at Philippi here,
Answering before we do demand of them.

Octavius tells Antony that instead of waiting in the hills, Brutus and Cassius are approaching with their armies. They plan to attack them at Philippi, even before Octavius and Antony can begin the battle.

MESSENGER   Prepare you, generals.
The enemy comes on in gallant show.
Their bloody sign of battle is hung out,
And something to be done
immediately.

A messenger comes to warn Octavius and Antony that the enemy is approaching. Antony commands Octavius to take the left side of the field, but Octavius says he will take the right side, while Antony must take the left.

Brutus, Cassius, and their armies enter. The two army generals meet. They insult one another.

ANTONY   In your bad strokes, Brutus, you give good
words.
Witness the hole you made in Caesar's heart,
Crying "Long live, hail, Caesar!"

Antony accuses Brutus of cowardly killing Caesar while shouting praises to his long life. He reminds Brutus of how he shouted praises while piercing a hole in Caesar's heart.

CASSIUS   Antony,
The posture of your blows are yet unknown.
But for your words, they rob the Hybla bees
And leave them honeyless.

Cassius accuses Antony of being deceitful when he met the conspirators after Caesar's assassination. He says Antony's words are so sweet that they leave the Hybla bees without any honey.

ANTONY Villains, you did not so when your vile
daggers
Hacked one another in the sides of Caesar.
You showed your teeth like apes, and fawned
like hounds,
And bowed like bondmen, kissing Caesar's
feet,
Whilst damnèd Casca, like a cur behind
Struck Caesar on the neck. O you flatterers!

Antony calls the conspirators villains and says they flattered
Caesar. They smiled like apes and fawned like dogs all round
Caesar, bowing like slaves and kissing his feet, while Casca
stabbed Caesar in the neck from behind.

CASSIUS Flatterers!—Now, Brutus, thank yourself.
This tongue had not offended so today
If Cassius might have ruled.

Cassius is outraged by Antony's accusations. He reminds Brutus
that they would not have had to listen to Antony's offensive
words now, if he had died with Caesar. Cassius had warned
Brutus that Antony must not be allowed to live if Caesar was
killed. Now, Cassius tells Brutus that if he had listened to his
advice, they would not be insulted like this by Antony.

OCTAVIUS (draws his sword)

> Look, I draw a sword against conspirators.
> When think you that the sword goes up
> again?
> Never, till Caesar's three and thirty wounds
> Be well avenged, or till another Caesar
> Have added slaughter to the sword of traitors.

Octavius says that they should stop talking and begin fighting. He draws his sword and promises that he will not sheath his sword until either Caesar's death has been avenged or he has been killed by traitors.

OCTAVIUS

> Come, Antony, away.—
> Defiance, traitors, hurl we in your
> teeth.
> If you dare fight today, come to the
> field.
> If not, when you have stomachs.

Octavius defies Brutus and Cassius. He challenges Brutus and Cassius to bring their armies onto the battlefield and fight now or whenever they gather the courage. Octavius, Antony, and their armies leave.

CASSIUS   You know that I held Epicurus strong
            And his opinion. Now I change my mind,
            And partly credit things that do presage.
            Coming from Sardis, on our former ensign
            Two mighty eagles fell, and there they
            perched,
            Gorging and feeding from our soldiers'
            hands,
            Who to Philippi here consorted us.
            This morning are they fled away and gone,
            And their stead's do ravens, crows and kites
            Fly o'er our heads and downward look on us
            As we were sickly prey. Their shadows seem
            A canopy most fatal, under which
            Our army lies, ready to give up the ghost.

Cassius speaks to Messala and tells him that he has serious doubts about the battle that is to come. Cassius says he never believed in omens like Epicurus. But now, Cassius has changed his mind and tells Messala that he believes in omens.

He tells Messala that while they were traveling to Philippi from Sardis, two eagles perched on the flag that flew in front of the army. These eagles even ate from the soldiers' hands. But Cassius has noticed that the eagles have flown away. In their place, ravens, crows and kites fly overhead, looking down at Brutus and Cassius' armies as though they were prey.

The eagles signified victory in battle and were seen as a good omen. When Cassius sees that the eagles have abandoned them, he believes that they will not be successful in the battle. The ravens, crows and kites are birds of prey: scavengers that feed on dead corpses after a battle. The sight of these birds circling over their heads like a canopy of death means that Brutus and Cassius' armies will face defeat.

BRUTUS   **No, Cassius, no. Think not, thou noble Roman,**
                    That ever Brutus will go bound to Rome.
                    He bears too great a mind. But this same day
                    Must end that work the ides of March begun.

When Cassius asks Brutus what he would do if they lost the battle, Brutus says that he would never allow himself to be captured. Brutus rejects the idea of committing suicide because he finds it cowardly. He is too proud as a Roman to return to Rome as a captive. Brutus says that day's battle will finish the work they began on the ides of March.

BRUTUS   **And whether we shall meet again I know not.**
                    Therefore our everlasting farewell take.
                    Forever and forever farewell, Cassius.
                    If we do meet again, why, we shall smile.
                    If not, why then this parting was well made.

Brutus does not know if he and Cassius will meet again. They bid each other farewell and promise that if they do meet again, they will smile.

SCENE 2

The battle of Philippi has begun.

BRUTUS   Let them set on at once, for I perceive
But cold demeanor in Octavius' wing,
And sudden push gives them the overthrow
Ride, ride, Messala. Let them all come down.

Brutus sends Messala with a message to Cassius. Brutus thinks Octavius' army is weakening. He urges Cassius to launch a surprise attack on the enemy.

SCENE 3

On another part of the battlefield, Cassius sees his men retreating.

CASSIUS **O, look, Titinius, look, the villains fly!**
Myself have to mine own turned enemy.
This ensign here of mine was turning back.
I slew the coward and did take it from him.

Seeing his men retreating, Cassius complains that he has become an enemy to his own soldiers. Cassius says he saw his cowardly standard bearer fleeing so he killed him and took the flag from him.

Titinius tells Cassius that Brutus commanded them to attack too early. Brutus' men have driven away Octavius' army. Brutus' soldiers are looking around the field for spoils of war. Now Cassius was surrounded by Antony's army.

Cassius' servant Pindarus comes to tell his master that Antony's army is approaching. He asks Cassius to flee.

CASSIUS   Titinius, if thou lovest me,
Mount thou my horse, and hide thy spurs in him
Till he have brought thee up to yonder troops
And here again, that I may rest assured
Whether yond troops are friend or enemy.

Cassius sees his tents on fire and sends Titinius to ride toward the soldiers in the distance. He asks Titinius to find out if those soldiers were from the enemy army.

PINDARUS   (above)
Titinius is enclosèd round about
With horsemen, that make to him on the spur.
Yet he spurs on. Now they are almost on him.
Now, Titinius. Now some light. Oh, he lights too.
He's ta'en.

Cassius asks Pindarus to climb to the top of the hill and watch Titinius. Pindarus tells Cassius that he saw Titinius get off from his horse in the midst of soldiers who were shouting with joy.

CASSIUS   Oh, coward that I am, to live so long
                    To see my best friend ta'en before my face!

Cassius believes that Titinius has been captured by the enemy. He laments that he was a coward to live so long to see his friend captured by the enemy. Cassius realizes that he will soon be captured by Antony and Octavius and dragged through the streets of Rome in chains.

CASSIUS   Come hither, sirrah,
                    In Parthia did I take thee prisoner.
                    And then I swore thee, saving of thy life,
                    That whatsoever I did bid thee do,
                    Thou shouldst attempt it. Come now, keep
                    thine oath.
                    Now be a free man, and with this good sword
                    That ran through Caesar's bowels, search this
                    bosom.
                    Stand not to answer. Here take thou the hilts
                    And, when my face is covered, as 'tis now,
                    Guide thou the sword.

Cassius reminds Pindarus of the oath he made to Cassius when Cassius saved his life in Parthia. Cassius now asks Pindarus to honor that promise and stab him with his sword. He gives his servant his sword and Pindarus stabs Cassius.

CASSIUS   Caesar, thou art revenged,
                    Even with the sword that killed thee.

Cassius dies saying that Caesar's death has been avenged with the same sword that killed him.

MESSALA   It is but change, Titinius, for Octavius
              Is overthrown by noble Brutus' power,
              As Cassius' legions are by Antony.

Titinius and Messala arrive to tell Cassius the good news that Octavius' army was overthrown by Brutus at the same time that Antony attacked Cassius' army.

Pindarus made a huge mistake when he told Cassius that Titinius had been captured by the enemy. Titinius was not captured. He was welcomed by some of Brutus' soldiers when he approached on horseback.

Titinius and Messala find Cassius' dead body.

TITINIUS   No, this was he, Messala,
               But Cassius is no more. O setting sun,
               As in thy red rays thou dost sink tonight,
               So in his red blood Cassius' day is set.
               The sun of Rome is set. Our day is gone.
               Clouds, dews, and dangers come! Our deeds
               are done.
               Mistrust of men success hath done this deed.

Titinius grieves when he finds Cassius dead. He says just like the sun's rays turn red at sunset, Cassius too has ended his life in a pool of red blood. Titinius says the sun of Rome has set because Rome has lost a noble soldier. Titinius says that Cassius killed himself because he did not believe that Titinius would return.

MESSALA Mistrust of good success hath done this deed.
O hateful error, melancholy's child,
Why doesn't thou show to the apt thoughts of men
The things that are not? O error, soon conceived,
Thou never comes unto a happy birth
But kill'st the mother that engendered thee!

Messala says that Cassius killed himself because he thought that they had lost the battle. His sadness gave way to his mistaken thinking which led to his death.

MESSALA Seek him, Titinius, whilst I go to meet
The noble Brutus, thrusting this report
Into his ears. I may say "thrusting" it,
For piercing steel and darts envenomèd
Shall be as welcome to the ears of Brutus
As tidings of this sight.

Messala tells Titinius to search for Pindarus while he goes to inform Brutus of Cassius' death. Messala says he will have to force the news into Brutus' ears because hearing this sad news will be like piercing steel and poisoned darts into Brutus' ears.

TITINIUS   Why didst thou send me forth, brave Cassius?
Did I not meet thy friends? And did not they
Put on my brows this wreath of victory
And bid me give it thee? Didst thou not hear
their shouts?
Alas, thou hast misconstrued everything!
But, hold thee, take this garland on thy brow.
Thy Brutus bid me give it thee, and I
Will do his bidding.

Titinius mourns Cassius' death. Titinius asks his dead friend if he did not see that he had been welcomed by friends and not enemies. Titinius tells Cassius that Brutus' soldiers had placed a wreath of victory on his head. Brutus had given Titinius a wreath to give to Cassius. Titinius mourns that Cassius did not hear the shouts of victory. He says his friend had misunderstood everything. Titinius places the wreath of victory on Cassius' head just as Brutus had told him to do.

TITINIUS   Come, Cassius' sword, and find Titinius'
heart.

Titinius then takes Cassius' sword and stabs himself.

Brutus arrives with Messala, Young Cato, Strato, Volumnius, and Lucilius. They find the lifeless bodies of Titinius and Cassius.

BRUTUS   **Friends, I owe more tears**
To this dead man than you shall see me pay.
—I shall find time, Cassius, I shall find time.

Brutus bids both Cassius and Titinius a sad farewell. He looks at Cassius' body and says that he has many more tears to mourn the death of Cassius than he will be able to shed there on the battlefield. He promises that he will find time to grieve for Cassius. The men leave to launch another attack on the enemy.

SCENE 4

Brutus arrives on the battlefield with Young Cato, Lucilius, and others while the fighting is in progress.

BRUTUS   **Yet, countrymen, O, yet hold up your heads!**

Brutus encourages his soldiers to continue the fight bravely. He retreats from the battlefield.

YOUNG CATO   **What bastard doth not? Who will go with me?**
I will proclaim my name about the field.
I am the son of Marcus Cato , ho!
A foe to tyrants, and my country's friend.
I am the son of Marcus Cato, ho!

Young Cato asks the soldiers, who among them will not follow him into battle. He shouts his name, saying he is the son of Marcus Cato. Young Cato proclaims his loyalty to Rome.

LUCILIUS **And I am Brutus, Marcus Brutus, I!**
Brutus, my country's friend. Know me for
Brutus!

In the fight that follows, Young Cato is killed. Lucilius is captured by Antony's soldiers who think that he is Brutus.

LUCILIUS **Only I yield to die.**
There is so much that thou wilt kill me
straight.
Kill Brutus, and be honored in his death.

When the soldiers demand that Lucilius must surrender or die, he refuses to surrender. Lucilius says that he would prefer to die. He gives the soldiers money to kill him immediately. He says they will find honor in killing Brutus. However, the soldiers recognize that he is a noble prisoner and do not kill him.

When Antony arrives, the soldiers tell him that they have captured Brutus. Antony immediately realizes that the prisoner his soldiers have captured is not Brutus. He asks Lucius where Brutus is.

LUCILIUS Safe, Antony. Brutus is safe enough.
I dare assure thee that no enemy
Shall ever take alive the noble Brutus.
The gods defend him from so great a shame!
When you do find him, or alive or dead,
He will be found like Brutus, like himself.

Lucilius tells Antony that Brutus is alive. He says Brutus will never be captured alive by the enemy, because to be captured is a shame. He tells Antony that Brutus will decide when and how he must be found.

ANTONY (to soldiers)
This is not Brutus, friend, but I assure you,
A prize no less in worth. Keep this man safe.
Give him all kindness. I had rather have
Such men my friends than enemies. Go on,
And see whether Brutus be alive or dead.
And bring us word unto Octavius' tent
How everything is chanced.

Antony is impressed by Lucilius' bravery and loyalty to his master. He commands his soldiers to guard Lucilius and treat him well. Antony sends his soldiers to search for Brutus, to find out whether he is alive or dead. He tells them to report to him later in Octavius' tent.

SCENE 5

Brutus, Dardanius, Clitus, Strato, and Volumnius gather near a rock. They are tired from the battle.

Brutus does not want to be captured. He whispers a request first to Clitus and then to Dardanius. He asks each of them if they will agree to kill him. They both refuse.

BRUTUS   **Why this, Volumnius**
              The ghost of Caesar hath appeared to me
              Two several times by night. At Sardis once,
              And this last night here in Philippi fields.
              I know my hour is come.

Brutus tells Volumnius that he has seen Caesar's ghost at night on two occasions: once in Sardis and a second time the previous night in the fields of Philippi. Brutus realizes that it is time for him to die. Volumnius disagrees, but Brutus insists, saying that the enemy has surrounded them.

BRUTUS   Good Volumnius,
Thou know'st that we two went to school
together.
Even for that our love of old, I prithee,
Hold thou my sword hilts, whilst I run on it.

Brutus asks Volumnius to hold his sword while he runs onto it. Volumnius refuses. He says that it is not something a friend should have to do.

The soldiers hear the sounds of battle and know that the enemy is approaching. Clitus warns Brutus to escape.

Brutus bids his companions farewell, saying they should go ahead and that he will follow.

BRUTUS   I prithee, Strato, stay thou by thy lord.
Thou art a fellow of good respect.
Thy life hath had some smatch of honor in it.
Hold then my sword and turn away thy face
While I do run upon it. Wilt thou, Strato?

Strato stays behind with Brutus. Brutus now asks Strato to hold his sword and look away, while he runs onto it. He says Strato will agree to do this if he is a respectable man. Strato agrees to hold Brutus' sword. The two men shake hands in farewell.

BRUTUS   Caesar, now be still.
               I killed not thee with half so good a will.

As Brutus runs onto his sword, he calls out that Caesar's spirit can now rest. Brutus says he did not kill Caesar as willingly as he is killing himself.

Octavius, Antony, Messala, Lucilius, and the army enter.

They find Strato with Brutus' lifeless body. Octavius offers to take all Brutus' men into his service.

ANTONY   This was the noblest Roman of them
                    all.
                    All the conspirators save only he
                    Did that they did in envy of great
                    Caesar.
                    He only, in a general honest thought
                    And common good to all, made one of
                    them.
                    His life was gentle, and the elements
                    So mixed in him that Nature might
                    stand up
                    And say to all the world "This was a
                    man!"

Antony delivers a poignant speech over Brutus' body. He says Brutus was the most noble Roman. Antony has realized that all the other conspirators attacked Caesar because they were jealous of him. Antony says of all the conspirators, only Brutus killed Caesar because he believed that his death would be for the good of Rome.

OCTAVIUS According to his virtue let us use him,
With all respect and rites of burial.
Within my tent his bones tonight shall
lie
Most like a soldier, ordered honorably.
So call the field to rest, and let's away
To part the glories of this happy day.

Octavius promises that Brutus will be given an honorable funeral. Octavius says Brutus' body will lie in his tent for the night. He orders the soldiers to end the battle and join in the victory celebration.

... ...

ABOUT THE AUTHOR

DHEERAJ KAPOOR has been drawn to books and the English language from a young age. After pursuing a Bachelor of Arts Honors Degree in English Studies, he discovered a passion for teaching.

An alumni of Vidyashilp Academy, Bangalore, Dheeraj has also compiled and published Study Guides to *A Midsummer Night's Dream* and *The Merchant of Venice* by William Shakespeare.

Dheeraj lives in Bangalore, India. You can follow his academic endeavors on https://syllableblog.wordpress.com

Printed in Great Britain
by Amazon

83464189R00068